This painting hangs in the lobby of the Legislative Council of the Parliament of New South Wales. It is called *The Founding of Australia by Capt. Arthur Phillip RN Sydney Cove Jan 26th, 1788*. A British painter, Algernon Talmage RA, made it in 1937.

The painting depicts the flag-raising ceremony at Sydney Cove on 26 January 1788. *Supply* rides at anchor in Sydney Cove, while Captain Arthur Phillip, the first Governor of New South Wales, in a blue jacket in the centre of the painting, raises a glass to make a toast. Among the other officers in the painting are the Judge Advocate, Captain David Collins, Lieutenant Philip Gidley King and the

Master of *Supply*, Commander H.L. Ball.[1]

A well-known Sydney businessman, Frank Albert, commissioned the painting as a Coronation Gift for King George VI in 1937. The painting that was given to the King hangs in the Tate Gallery, in London. A second version of the painting was commissioned for the New South Wales Parliament. The State Library of New South Wales holds an oil sketch of the painting, made in 1937.[2]

---

1 Talmage made notes on the back of the paintings identifying the main subjects.

2 *Catalogue of the State Library of New South Wales*, Call number ML 1222. See also https://www.tate.org.uk/art/artworks/talmage-the-founding-of-australia-1788-n04877, visited 15 June 2020.

Does 26 January 1788 Matter?

Fact, Fiction and the Founding of Australia

RICHARD TRAVERS

Australian Scholarly

First published 2020 by
Australian Scholarly Publishing Ltd
7 Lt Lothian St Nth, North Melbourne, Vic 3051
Tel: 03 9329 6963 / Fax: 03 9329 5452
enquiry@scholarly.info / www.scholarly.info

ISBN 978-1-922454-15-7

Cover design: Wayne Saunders

Contents

Celebrating the anniversary of 26 January
1788 1 • What will be argued 6 • Sydney
before January 1788 8 • European power 9 •
European State practice 10 • *Terra Australis
Incognita* 16 • The decision to establish a
penal colony in New South Wales 20 • Events
at Sydney on 26 January 1788 23 • Events
at Sydney on 7 February 1788 28 • Legal
and constitutional significance 33 • Justice
Windeyer's arguments 36 • When did
English law become the territorial law of
the colony? 37 • *Mabo v Queensland [No 2]*
(1991–1992) 175 CLR 1 42 • When was the
colony of New South Wales founded? 45 • The
documents establishing the colony 48 • Phillip's
commissions 48 • Phillip's instructions 50
• What legal or constitutional significance
attaches to the events of 26 January 1788? 52
• Founding Australia? 53 • Reconciliation
57 • When, or what, should we celebrate
as Australia Day? 59 • Bibliography 61

Celebrating the anniversary of 26 January 1788

The anniversary of 26 January 1788 was celebrated from the time of Governor Macquarie. It was called Anniversary Day. Typical was the party on 26 January 1825, when a group of 'currency lads and emancipists' met at Hill's Hotel to celebrate the 37th anniversary of the colony. Currency lads and lasses were native-born, non-indigenous Australians; emancipists were convicts who had been pardoned, or whose sentences had expired.[3] W.C. Wentworth was their leader. They drank many toasts, including to Governor Phillip, to Macquarie, to trial by jury, to freedom of the press and to: 'The land, boys, we live in'.[4]

By 1830, the Anniversary Day celebration had become an occasion to speak out against tyranny, both in the colony and the Mother Country. A toast to W.C. Wentworth, 'the single-handed patriot of Australia', was met with deafening cheers.[5]

1838 marked the 50th anniversary of the colony. There

3　Bruce (ed) Moore, *The Australian National Dictionary Australian Words and Their Origins* (Melbourne: Australian National University and Oxford University Press, 2016), 458 and 564.

4　C.M.H. Clark, *A History of Australia, Volume 2: New South Wales and Van Diemen's Land 1822–1838* (Melbourne: Melbourne University Press, 1968), 55.

5　Ibid., 97. Matthew Flinders and Macquarie were two who popularised the name *Australia*.

were church services, a regatta on Sydney Harbour, but the celebration had lost its radical edge. After the traditional toast to 'The land, boys, we live in', the band played *God Save the Queen*, the men toasted Queen Victoria. While the band played Hail Australia, they toasted the sister colonies, Van Diemen's Land and South Australia.[6]

Manning Clark regarded the celebrations of Anniversary Day as a barometer of an emerging Australian sensibility that developed gradually after white settlement. By 1850, the elements of the sensibility were: the ascendancy of the white settler; the acceptance and observation of Christian ethics; the abolition of convict transportation; the establishment of schools and universities; the emergence of industries to complement agriculture as a source of colonial wealth; the use of railways and faster shipping to speed goods to markets; and the introduction of legislative councils.[7] In short, the Australian sensibility was based entirely on British values and aspirations. It excluded indigenous people.

The celebrations of Anniversary Day celebrated, not so much the past, as the future. Rather than concentrating on the landing at Sydney Cove, or the convict past, the focus of the celebrations came to be Australia, the qualities that

---

6   C.M.H. Clark, *A History of Australia, Volume 3: The Beginning of an Australian Civilization 1824–1851* (Melbourne: Melbourne University Press, 1973), 139.

7   Ibid., For the elements, see: Chapter 15 Tethering the Mighty Bush to the World, page 405ff. The quotation is on page 448.

made it great, and its prospects for the future. Moreover, the sensibility was not static. It changed over time.

26 January 1888 would mark the centenary of white settlement, or, as the *Bulletin* called it, 'the day we were lagged.'[8] Whatever the day meant for New South Wales, it meant little to the other Australian colonies. They were happy to leave it to New South Wales to celebrate on its own.

Left to his own devices, Henry Parkes, the Premier of New South Wales proposed to celebrate the centenary by changing the name of New South Wales to Australia. In the resulting uproar, other Premiers wrote indignantly to the Colonial Secretary in London. They complained that Parkes was stealing a name that rightly belonged to the entire continent. With the help of Lord Carrington, the Governor of New South Wales, and the promise of a knighthood, the Colonial Secretary persuaded Parkes that the name Australia was not his to appropriate.[9]

The name Australia was, therefore, available when Sir

8   A.W. Martin, *Henry Parkes: A Biography* (Melbourne: Melbourne University Press, 1980), 368. 'Lagged' was a slang term for transporting a convict to a penal settlement in Australia: Moore, *The Australian National Dictionary Australian Words and Their Origins*, 862–863.

9   Martin, *Henry Parkes: A Biography*, 368–369. Helen Irving, *The Centenary Companion to Australian Federation* (Cambridge ; Melbourne: Cambridge University Press, 1999), 30. The other self-governing colonies were Victoria, Queensland, South Australia and Tasmania. Western Australia did not gain the right of self-government until 1890.

Henry Parkes swung his considerable influence behind federation, and it was Parkes who suggested the name. The British Parliament duly passed the *Commonwealth of Australia Constitution Act* which created a 'Federal Commonwealth under the name of the *Commonwealth of Australia*'.[10] Federation delivered something that remains unique on earth: a nation for a continent and a continent for a nation.

The Commonwealth of Australia was inaugurated on 1 January 1901. The date was chosen deliberately – it was the first day of the new century. Now that Australia existed, there could be an Australia Day, but the opportunity to celebrate it on 1 January was ignored in favour of continued celebration on 26 January. One of the fathers of federation, Alfred Deakin, wrote of 26 January 1906 that:

> Our national holiday was observed this year with Australian wholeheartedness, but with a scant allowance of ceremony. What there was of that was English. We are miserable copyists in all such matters, and a luncheon with speeches marks the limit of our invention in the way of formal demonstrations. The first settlement in Australia and the foundation of

---

10 JA La Nauze, 'The Name of the Commonwealth of Australia', *Australian Historical Studies* 15 (1971). *Commonwealth of Australia Constitution Act* (1900) (Imp), s3.

New South Wales are honoured in this same fashion on January 26 each twelvemonths with deadly earnestness and on most occasions deadly dullness … To us our celebration marks little more than another holiday …[11]

The anniversary of 26 January 1788 continued to be celebrated, but not as Australia Day. It went under a variety of names, including Anniversary Day, Foundation Day, First Landing Day, and, in Victoria, A.N.A, Day, after the Australian Natives' Association, which promoted the event. It was not until the 1930s that the anniversary came to be called Australia Day across the country.[12]

The Tate loaned its version of the Talmage painting to the Australian Government for the celebrations of the 150th anniversary of 26 January 1788. The celebrations centred on Sydney, as might be expected. The New South Wales Art Gallery squeezed 826 works into an exhibition of *150 Years of Australian Art*.[13] The Lord Mayor of Sydney erected a commemorative plaque in the entrance foyer of Sydney Town Hall that proclaimed:

11 Alfred Deakin, *Federated Australia* (Melbourne: Melbourne University Press, 1968), 171.

12 K.S. Inglis, 'Australia Day', *Australian Historical Studies* 13, no. 49 (1967).

13 *150 Years of Australian Art*, National Art Gallery of New South Wales.

This tablet was erected by
the Municipal Council of Sydney
to commemorate the
150th anniversary of the
foundation of Australia
at Sydney 26 Jan. 1788

Alderman Norman L. Nock
Lord Mayor

Frank Albert commissioned Talmage to make a second copy of his painting of 26 January 1788, and gave it to the New South Wales Parliament, where it hangs today.

What will be argued

26 January has no claim to be celebrated as Australia Day.

Australia was not founded at Sydney on 26 January 1788, neither was the colony of New South Wales.

The events that took place at Sydney on 26 January 1788 signify little and are unworthy of celebration. What appears in Talmage's painting to be an occasion of some formality was, in fact, a drinks party given by Governor Phillip for a few officers and men of the *Supply* to celebrate their safe arrival in Sydney and to toast the success of the colony they were about to establish.

Those who thought that the colony of New South Wales was founded in 1788 and the Commonwealth of Australia was founded in 1901 may be surprised to learn that installations in Australia's senior Parliament and in Sydney Town Hall claim that Australia was founded at Sydney on 26 January 1788. The claim is not valid.

Sir Victor Windeyer, a Justice of the High Court of Australia and a legal historian, claimed that the events depicted in the Talmage painting marked the foundation of the colony of New South Wales, and the 'reassertion and … making good of the title of the British Crown to the territory of which Cook had already formally taken possession in the name of the King.'[14] They did not. Still less did they mark the founding of Australia.

26 January lacks, and always lacked, genuine national significance. If it remains on the national calendar, it should be as a day of reconciliation.

Let it be supposed that the national day of a country should reflect its values, ambitions, and aspirations. Let it be supposed that Australia Day should celebrate the diversity of its migrant population. Let it be supposed that Australia Day is for all Australians to celebrate. If this is what Australia Day should be, we would better celebrate it on almost any

14 The Honourable Sir Victor Windeyer, '"A Birthright and Inheritance" the Establishment of the Rule of Law in Australia', *(1958–63) 1 Tasmanian University Law Review 635* (1961): 637.

day of the year, except 26 January.

Inclusion demands a better response.

Sydney before January 1788

Sydney is the British name for a part of the Australian continent that was, before British settlement, the territory of indigenous people. In the area of Botany Bay, Port Jackson, and Broken Bay, the Cammeraygal were dominant. Cammeraygal territory was on the North Shore of Sydney Harbour. Sydney Cove was in Gadigal territory. Gadigal territory ran from South Head almost to Sydney Airport and west to Petersham.[15] The indigenous population was sparse. Governor Phillip estimated that the total population of the indigenous people of Botany Bay, Port Jackson and Broken Bay area was in the order of 1,400 to 1,600 people.[16]

The indigenous people pursued a way of life that eschewed

---

15 David Collins, *An Account of the English Colony in New South Wales* (Sydney: AH & AW Reed 1975), Volume 1, page 453. John Hunter, *An Historical Journal of Events at Sydney and at Sea 1787–1792* (Sydney: Angus & Robertson, 1968), 274–275. See also: Keith Willey, *When the Sky Fell Down: The Destruction of the Tribes of the Sydney Region 1788–1850s* (Sydney: Collins, 1979), 14–15.; Inga Clendinnen, *Dancing with Strangers* (Melbourne: Text Publishing, 2003), 290–291.

16 This was Governor Phillip's estimate: *Dancing with Strangers*, 26. The original of Phillip's letter in which he gives the estimate is in the Mitchell Library: Ms C213 (Clendinnen, 294).

possessions and permanent housing. Until January 1788, they lived undisturbed and isolated from the outside world.

European power

The development of European sea power from the 15th century transformed the Atlantic Ocean into a giant marketplace. European nations sold finished goods to Africa and the New World; traders (mostly European) acquired slaves in Africa for sale in the New World; and the New World produced gold, silver, and agricultural products for sale in Europe.

Inequality and exploitation were hallmarks of the market, seen most vividly in the slave trade. Quite apart from slavery, the establishment of Spanish and Portuguese colonies in South America and British colonies in North America displaced indigenous populations. Factors including dominant technologies (steel and weaponry) and the spread of European diseases (smallpox, measles, influenza, and venereal diseases) gave the Europeans a competitive advantage over indigenous populations. These factors often meant that the Europeans were able to overcome indigenous populations without the need to conquer them.

The European experience of the Atlantic trade created a habit of thinking that could readily evolve. If Europeans could dominate the Americas, why not elsewhere?

European State practice

In support of their ambitions, the European powers agreed among themselves how they would divide the territories they discovered outside Europe. This combination, formed without the knowledge or consent of the inhabitants of the territories that were divided, was so presumptuous that the great American jurist, Chief Justice John Marshall, made fun of it in his judgment in *Worcester v Georgia* 31 U.S. 515 (1832):

> America, separated from Europe by a wide ocean, was inhabited by a distinct people, divided into separate nations, independent of each other and of the rest of the world, having institutions of their own, and governing themselves by their own laws. It is difficult to comprehend the proposition, that the inhabitants of either quarter of the globe could have rightful original claims of dominion over the inhabitants of the other, or over the lands they occupied; or that the discovery of either by the other should give the discoverer rights in the country discovered, which annulled the pre-existing rights of its ancient possessors.

After lying concealed for a series of ages, the enterprise of Europe, guided by nautical science, conducted some of her adventurous sons into the western world. They found it in possession of a people who had made small progress in agriculture or manufactures, and whose general employment was war, hunting, and fishing.[17]

Chief Justice Marshall questioned how these adventurers could acquire 'a rightful property' in the land they discovered simply by sailing along its coast and occasionally landing, but he recognised that 'power, war, conquest, give rights, which, after possession, are conceded by the world.'[18]

In this, the Chief Justice was adopting an argument that Queen Elizabeth I had made in 1561 when the King of Portugal complained to her that some of her subjects had landed on parts of the coast of West Africa that the Portuguese had claimed but not occupied. The Queen informed the Portuguese that the Crown would:

… restrain its subjects from 'haunting any new-found land' wherein the King of Portugal had 'obedience, dominion and tribute,' but

---

17 *Worcester v Georgia* 31 U.S. 515 (1832), at 542–543.

18 *Worcester v Georgia*, at 543.

would not recognize his sovereignty in 'places discovered whereof he had no superiority at all.' In other words, [Queen Elizabeth I] maintained that effective occupation gave a valid title, but discovery did not.[19]

Chief Justice Marshall described the combination of the European powers as follows:

> To avoid bloody conflicts, which might terminate disastrously to all, it was necessary for the nations of Europe to establish some principle which all would acknowledge, and which should decide their respective rights as between themselves. This principle, suggested by the actual state of things, was, 'that discovery gave title to the government by whose authority it was made, against all other European governments, which title might be consummated by possession.'

This principle, acknowledged by all Europeans,

---

19 Ernest Scott, 'Taking Possession of Australia – the Doctrine of "Terra Nullius" (No-Man's Land)', *Royal Australian Historical Society Journal and Proceedings* 26 (1940): 4. The combination was a matter of State practice – to be effective, the various States had all to honour the principle behind the agreement.

because it was in the interests of all to acknowledge it, gave to the nation making the discovery, as its inevitable consequence, the sole right of acquiring the soil and of making settlements on it. It was an exclusive principle which shut out the right of competition among those who agreed to it; not one which could annul the previous rights of those who had not agreed to it. It regulated the right given by discovery among the European discoverers; but could not affect the rights of those already in possession, either as aboriginal occupants, or as occupants by virtue of a discovery made before the memory of man.[20]

In this context, of course, the word *discovery* makes sense only if used from a European perspective. The American continent had been inhabited for thousands of years by people for whom its existence would not have been a discovery. In similar fashion, *Far East* only makes sense from a European perspective. For Australians, the Far East is the Near North.

Justice Brennan cited Chief Justice Marshall's judgment in support of the following passage from his judgment in *Mabo v Queensland [No 2]*:

---

20 *Worcester v Georgia*, at 543–544.

The great voyages of European discovery opened to European nations the prospect of occupying new and valuable territories that were already inhabited. As among themselves, the European nations parcelled out the territories newly discovered to the sovereigns of the respective discoverers, provided the discovery was confirmed by occupation and provided the indigenous inhabitants were not organized in a society that was united permanently for political action. To these territories the European colonial nations applied the doctrines relating to acquisition of territory that was *terra nullius*. They recognized the sovereignty of the respective European nations over the territory of 'backward peoples' and, by State practice, permitted the acquisition of sovereignty of such territory by occupation rather than by conquest.[21]

Whilst the European nations agreed amongst themselves the terms on which they would appropriate other countries, they did not ask the inhabitants of those other countries if

---

21 *Mabo v Queensland [No 2]* (1991–1992) 175 CLR 1, Brennan J at 32. *Terra nullius* means 'land belonging to no-one': Moore, *The Australian National Dictionary Australian Words and Their Origins*, 1592.

they agreed to be bound by the European rules. As Professor Scott put it:

> Little regard was paid to the rights of original inhabitants by any of the colonizing peoples. Generally, they considered that they were acting righteously in introducing the Christian religion to lands previously heathen.[22]

Although this practice was expedient (and even justified) in European eyes, taking sovereignty of the territory of others without their consent raises questions of legitimacy, especially when the takers claim to observe and uphold the rule of law – and expect others to do likewise.

As cosy as the combination may have been for the European powers, the process of acquiring title to territory under the combination had its complications. In practice, it was a three-stage process, involving: (i) discovering and mapping territory that qualified as *terra nullius*; (ii) claiming possession of it; and (iii) occupying it. The claim of possession was a simple ceremony carried out by the explorer at the

---

22 Scott, 'Taking Possession of Australia – the Doctrine of "Terra Nullius" (No-Man's Land)', 4. Professor Scott was prompted to look into the doctrine of Terra Nullius because he believed that, in 1939, the United States was considering invoking it to take possession of parts of Antarctica to defeat possible incursions there by Nazi Germany: pages 2–3.

point of the discovery. Performed, in most cases, with no outside witnesses, the claim was a form of words – a gesture in colonialism. Sometimes a flag was raised. Sometimes a marker was left. The explorer would claim possession of the territory for his monarch but seldom, if ever, take actual possession of it. And actual possession was the key. The claim would fall away if another European nation occupied the territory before the discovering nation.[23]

Terra Australis Incognita

Terra Australis Incognita – the unknown southern land – also known as *New Holland* first appeared on European maps after Dutch sailors discovered different parts of it in the first half of the 17th century.[24] The northern and western parts, that the Dutch had found, were on the maps, but most of the south coast and the east coast remained uncharted.

In 1768, the government of King George III of England sent Captain James Cook to Tahiti. Cook's primary task was a scientific mission – to observe the transit of Venus. Cook's orders were to return home via the Cape of Good Hope,

---

23 Ibid.

24 Robert Clancy, *The Mapping of Terra Australis* (Sydney: Universal Press Pty Limited, 1995), 72ff. Willem Jansz discovered the west coast of Cape York Peninsula; Dirck Hartog, the west coast; Jan Carstensz, Arnhem Land; and Abel Tasman, New Zealand and Tasmania. Tasman also circumnavigated Australia.

charting a course through the south Pacific that would have to intersect, at some point, with the east coast of *Terra Australis Incognita*.

Cook succeeded in both tasks. Observing the transit of Venus from different places on the Earth's surface might make possible the calculation of the distance from the Earth to the Sun. Finding the east coast of *Terra Australis* might make available new territories for addition to the British Empire.

Cook did more on his journey than discover the east coast of *Terra Australis*. He mapped and claimed possession of the Society Islands (on 29 July 1769), the North Island of New Zealand (on 15 November 1769) and the South Island (on 31 January 1770). On each occasion, he conducted a small ceremony at which he hoisted the Union Jack and made the claim. The South Island ceremony took place at Queen Charlotte's Sound, named in honour of the Queen. On that account, Cook made an addition to the ceremony. He 'drank Her Majestys hilth in a Bottle of wine and gave the empty bottle to the old man (who had attended us up the hill) with which he was highly pleased.' Cook recorded the details of each of these ceremonies in his journal.[25]

---

25 Captain James Cook, *The Journals of Captain James Cook on His Voyages of Discovery: The Voyage of the Endeavour 1768–1771*, ed. J.C. Beaglehole (Great Britain: The Boydell Press in association with Hordern House, Sydney, 1955), Society Islands, 144; North Island, 204; and South Island, 243.

Cook ran into the east coast of Australia on 17 April 1770 at Latitude 38°S, not far south of the border between New South Wales and Victoria. He spent a week in April exploring Botany Bay and its surroundings, recording in his journal that, 'During our stay in this Harbour I caused the English Colours to be display'd ashore every day and an inscription to be cut out upon one of the trees near the watering place setting forth the Ships name, date &c.' Although Cook noted that he displayed the flag every day, he did not record that he claimed possession of the land he had then discovered, although it is likely that he did, having regard to the entry he made in his journal when he claimed possession of the east coast on 22 August 1788.[26]

Leaving Botany Bay, Cook sailed north, mapping the coast to its northern-most point, Cape York. On 22 August 1770, Cook went ashore on an island in the Torres Strait that he named Possession Island. He was looking for a passage to the west, which, he hoped, would lead to Batavia (modern Jakarta). From a hill on the island, Cook found a passage through which he resolved to take his ship. That would mean leaving the east coast of *Terra Australis*. Cook wrote in his journal:

> Having satisfied myself of the great Probability

---

26 Ibid., 304–313. See also: Scott, 'Taking Possession of Australia – the Doctrine of "Terra Nullius" (No-Man's Land)'.

of a Passage, thro' which I intend going with the Ship, and therefore may land no more upon this Eastern Coast of *New Holland*, and on the Western side I can make no new discovery the honour of which [discovery] belongs to the Dutch navigators; but the Eastern Coast from the Latitude of 38°S down to this place I am confident was never seen or visited by any European before us, and Notwithstanding I had in the name of His Majesty taken possession of several places upon this coast, I now once more hoisted English Coulers and in the Name of His Majesty King George the Third, took possession of the whole Eastern Coast from the above Latitude [38°S] down to this place [Possession Island] by the name of *New South Wales* together with all the Bays, Harbours, Rivers and Islands situate upon the said coast, after which we fired three Volleys of small Arms which were Answerd by the like number from the Ship.[27]

In this passage, Cook acknowledged the claim of the Dutch to have discovered the western parts of *New Holland*

27 Cook, *The Journals of Captain James Cook on His Voyages of Discovery: The Voyage of the Endeavour 1768–1771*, 387–388.

whilst carefully asserting his claim to have been the first European to visit its East coast from Latitude 38°S to Possession Island in the north. Although Cook wrote that he had 'taken possession of several places upon this coast' (meaning, probably, at Botany Bay), the ceremony on Possession Island is the only ceremony on the east coast of *New Holland* recorded in his journal. Cook wrote that he 'took possession' of the entire east coast of *New Holland* when all he did was 'claim possession' of it. No sooner had he made the claim than he sailed away.

Cook defined New South Wales by reference to two lines on the map: a line running north-south through Possession Island and the latitude of Point Hicks, 38°S. Latitude 38°S runs east-west across the State of Victoria, passing through Port Philip just south of Melbourne. The line running south from Possession Island intersects with latitude 38°S in Western Victoria, between Warrnambool and Melbourne. The maximum extent of Cook's claim was, therefore, all the land north-east of the two lines.

The decision to establish a penal colony in New South Wales

Nothing may have come of Cook's claim had Britain not lost its American colonies in 1783. If Britain wanted to keep exporting surplus criminals, it would have to find somewhere else to send them. New South Wales seemed good to fill the void.

In 1786, King George III commissioned Captain Phillip to be Governor of New South Wales.[28] He placed Phillip in command of a Fleet of 11 ships, around 300 seamen and 1,030 more or less reluctant passengers: 736 convicts (548 male and 188 female); 17 of their children; 211 marines and officers; 27 of their wives and 19 of their children; and an official party of 21.[29]

Phillip's orders were to lead the Fleet on a voyage halfway round the world and establish a penal colony at Botany Bay, in New South Wales. Phillip arrived in Botany Bay on 18 January 1788. He had gone ahead of the main Fleet in *Supply*, an armed tender which was smaller and faster than

---

28 Phillip was given two commissions: the first, dated 12 October 1786, was a single page military commission; the second, dated 2 April 1787, was a detailed civil commission running to six typed pages. They are reproduced in: *Historical Records of Australia*, ed. Frederick Watson (Melbourne 1914), Volume 1, Series 1, page 1 (first commission) and page 2 (second commission).

29 Each ship had a crew of up to 30 men: Philip Gidley King, *The Journal of Philip Gidley King: Lieutenant, Rn 1787–1790* (Sydney: Australian Documents Library, 1980), 5–6. To count the passengers requires a complex reconciliation of many primary sources. The figures quoted here are taken from the reconciliation made by Eris O'Brien: Eris O'Brien, *The Foundation of Australia (1786–1800) a Study in English Criminal Practice and Penal Colonization in the Eighteenth Century* (Sydney: Angus and Robertson, 1950), Appendix B, pages 279–284. For the numbers of male and female convicts, see: ibid., 286.

the rest of the First Fleet. The rest of the Fleet arrived in Botany Bay over the next two days.

To Phillip's disappointment, Botany Bay was quite unsuitable, even for a prison.[30] Phillip knew that Port Jackson was only 'a few Leagues to the Northward.'[31] Could it be a better prospect than Botany Bay? Leaving the Fleet in Botany Bay, where men were clearing ground in case the settlement had to be there, Phillip led a party north in three small boats. Early in the afternoon of 22 January, Phillip and his party sailed into Port Jackson where they found, 'the finest harbour in the world, in which a thousand sail of the line may ride in the most perfect security.'[32]

After exploring several coves, Phillip selected Sydney Cove as the site for the settlement because it had 'the finest spring of water', and because ships could anchor so close to the shore that quays could be built to unload even the largest vessels.[33] It was during this exploration, on 24 January 1788,

30 Anonymous, *The Voyage of Governor Phillip to Botany Bay with an Account of the Establishment of the Colonies of Port Jackson & Norfolk Island* (London: John Stockdale, 1789), 46–47.

31 Margaret Cameron-Ash, *Lying for the Admiralty* (Sydney: Rosenberg Publishing Pty Ltd, 2018), 168.(citing a letter from Phillip to the Home Office written in May 1878).

32 Anonymous, *The Voyage of Governor Phillip to Botany Bay with an Account of the Establishment of the Colonies of Port Jackson & Norfolk Island*, 47.

33 Ibid., 47–48.

that Phillip first set foot on Sydney Cove.[34] On 24 January, 'having sufficiently explored Port Jackson', Phillip returned to Botany Bay where he issued orders for the Fleet to sail to Port Jackson the next morning.[35]

25 January 1788 was blowing a gale, making it impossible for most of the ships to leave Botany Bay. The exception was *Supply*, in which Phillip sailed, leaving the remainder of the Fleet to follow under convoy of *Sirius* when the winds were calmer.[36]

Events at Sydney on 26 January 1788

On 26 January 1788, *Supply* lay anchored in Sydney Cove. Phillip and some of the officers and men accompanying him went ashore. While they explored the site of the settlement, Phillip ordered carpenters from *Supply* to strike a flagpole in

---

34 Phillip had a plaque struck to that effect, which was in the original Government House: George Mackaness, *Admiral Arthur Phillip: Founder of New South Wales 1738–1814* (Sydney: Angus & Robertson Limited 1937), a photograph of the plaque is facing page 144. The original plaque is in the Mitchell Library: call number LR22.

35 Anonymous, *The Voyage of Governor Phillip to Botany Bay with an Account of the Establishment of the Colonies of Port Jackson & Norfolk Island* 51.

36 John White, *Journal of a Voyage to New South Wales* (Sydney: Angus and Robertson, 1962), 111. Anonymous, *The Voyage of Governor Phillip to Botany Bay with an Account of the Establishment of the Colonies of Port Jackson & Norfolk Island* 54.

a clearing on the side of the Cove. There, later that evening, 'the colours were displayed on shore, and the Governor, with several of his principal officers and others, assembled round the flagstaff, drank the King's health, and success to the settlement, with all that display of form which on such occasions is esteemed propitious, because it enlivens the spirits, and fills the imagination with pleasing presages.'[37]

David Collins, the Judge Advocate of the colony, and Lieutenant Philip Gidley King were with Phillip on *Supply* and left eyewitness accounts of the ceremony. David Collins wrote:

> In the evening of this day the whole of the party that came round in the *Supply* were assembled at the point where they first landed in the morning, and on which the flag-pole had been purposely erected and an union jack displayed, when the marines fired several vollies; between which the governor and the officers who accompanied him drank the healths of his Majesty and the Royal Family, and success to the new colony. The day, which had been uncommonly fine, concluded with the safe arrival of the *Sirius* and the convoy

37 *The Voyage of Governor Phillip to Botany Bay with an Account of the Establishment of the Colonies of Port Jackson & Norfolk Island*, 58.

from Botany Bay – thus terminating the voyage with the same good fortune that had from its commencement been so conspicuously their friend and companion.[38]

King left two contradictory accounts of the day. The description in the unpublished version of King's journal was essentially the same as Collins':

> After noon the Union Jack was hoisted on shore & the Marines being drawn up under it, the Governor & Officers to the right, & the Convicts to the left, Their Majesties & the Prince of Wales health, with success to the colony, was drank in four glasses of Porter, after which a *feu de joie* was fired & the whole gave three cheers, which ceremony was also observed on board the *Supply*.[39]

The account in the published version of King's journal was slightly different:

> The next day at Day light the English colours

38 Collins, *An Account of the English Colony in New South Wales*, Volume 1, pages 4–5.

39 Mackaness, *Admiral Arthur Phillip: Founder of New South Wales 1738–1814*, 110–111.

were displayed on shore & possession was taken for His Majesty whose health, with the Queens, Prince of Wales & Success to the Colony was drank; a *feu de joie* was fired by a party of Marines & ye whole gave three cheers which was returned by the *Supply*. At Sun sett the *Sirius* & all the Convoy anchored here.[40]

All the other First Fleet diarists were travelling with *Sirius* and the rest of the Fleet. Watkin Tench, John Hunter and William Bradley did not mention the party, perhaps, because they arrived in Sydney Cove after it was over or, perhaps, because being on board ship, they did not know that it had happened. Surgeon Worgan wrote that:

> On the Evening of our Arrival (26th January 1788) The Governor & a Number of Officers assembled on Shore where they Displayed the British Flag and each Officer with a Heart glowing with Loyalty drank His Majesty's Health and Success to the Colony.[41]

---

40 King, *The Journal of Philip Gidley King: Lieutenant, Rn 1787–1790*, 36.

41 George B Worgan, *Journal of a First Fleet Surgeon* (Sydney: The Library Council of New South Wales in association with the Library of Australian History, 1978), 8.

Surgeon White wrote:

> The *Supply* had arrived the day before, and
> the governor, with every person that could be
> spared from the ship, were on shore, clearing
> the ground for the encampment. In the evening,
> when all the ships had anchored, the English
> colours were displayed; and at the foot of the
> flag-staff his Majesty's health, and success to
> the settlement, was drank by the governor,
> many of the principal officers and private men
> who were present upon the occasion.[42]

Lieutenant King's published account was out of step with
the other accounts. It placed the party at first light when all
the others placed it in the afternoon or evening and it was
the only account that mentioned taking possession.[43] None
of the other accounts (including King's unpublished account)
ascribed formal significance to the occasion. They treated it
as a pleasant interlude for the officers and crew of *Supply* to

---

42 White, *Journal of a Voyage to New South Wales*, 112–113.

43 For completeness, Judge Advocate Collins also mentioned taking
possession three years later in his journal entry for 26 January
1791: 'Our colours were hoisted in the redoubt, in commemoration
of the day on which formal possession was taken of the cove three
years before.' Collins, *An Account of the English Colony in New South
Wales*, 122.

celebrate their safe arrival in Sydney Cove, and to toast the success of the colony they were about to establish.

It is this drinks party that is the subject of Algernon Talmage's painting and of Alderman Nock's plaque. It is the event that they described as the founding of Australia.

Events at Sydney on 7 February 1788

The author of *The Voyage of Governor Phillip to Botany Bay* did not regard the party on 26 January 1788 as having any legal or constitutional significance. He was clear that the colony of New South Wales was founded in the formal sense on 7 February 1788.

He wrote that, 'From [26 January] to the end of the first week in February all was hurry and exertion. Those who gave orders and those who received them were equally occupied; nor is it easy to conceive a busier scene than this part of the coast exhibited during the continuance of these first efforts towards establishment.'[44]

On 7 February 1788, Phillip assembled the entire personnel of the colony – free and convict – to witness a ceremony that the author of *The Voyage of Governor Phillip to Botany Bay* described as follows:

---

44 Anonymous, *The Voyage of Governor Phillip to Botany Bay with an Account of the Establishment of the Colonies of Port Jackson & Norfolk Island*, 58.

The 7th February, 1788, was the memorable day which established a regular form of government on the coast of New South Wales. For obvious reasons, all possible solemnity was given to the proceedings necessary on this occasion. On a space previously cleared, the whole colony was assembled; the military drawn up, and under arms; the convicts stationed apart; and near the person of the Governor, those who were to hold the principal offices under him. The Royal Commission was then read by Mr D Collins, the Judge Advocate. By this instrument Arthur Phillip was constituted and appointed Captain General and Governor in Chief in and over the territory, called New South Wales …[45]

The descriptions of the events of 26 January and 7 February in *The Voyage of Governor Phillip to Botany Bay* convey a clear view of their relative significance. 26 January was casual. 7 February bristled with formalities. The drinks party was a chance for Phillip and the few companions who happened to be with him on *Supply* to celebrate their arrival, to drink to the King and the new colony, and to enliven their spirits. The assembly on 7 February 1788 was a solemn ceremony to mark the establishment of a regular form of government for

---

45 Ibid., 64–66.

the new colony, attended by all available personnel, at which the colony was established and all its officers were confirmed in the positions to which they had been appointed.

One important formality was to mark the extension of the territorial limits of the colony of New South Wales beyond those claimed by Cook. The tip of Cape York remained the northern boundary of the colony, but its western boundary had been pushed west to 135°E longitude and its southern boundary pushed south to latitude 43°39'S. The western boundary was now a line running north-south from the coast of the Northern Territory east of Darwin to the coast of South Australia west of Port Augusta. The southern boundary was now a line running east-west south of Tasmania, but through the middle of the south island of New Zealand. The colony consisted of all the land north-east of the two lines the land, and the adjacent islands, including so much of the islands of New Zealand as lay north of latitude 43°39'S.[46]

In preparation for the despatch of the First Fleet, in 1787, the British Parliament had passed a statute, *27 George III, c. 2*, establishing a criminal court for the colony. On 2 April 1787, the King granted Letters Patent creating a civil court for the colony. In the ceremony on 7 February 1788, these courts were formally established, their officers were appointed, and the office of Lieutenant Governor was filled:

---

46 Ibid., 65.

The act of Parliament establishing the courts of judicature was next read; and lastly, the patents under the great seal, empowering the proper persons to convene and hold those courts whenever the exigency should require. The Office of Lieutenant Governor was conferred on Major Ross, of the Marines. A triple discharge of musquetry concluded this part of the ceremony …[47]

Finally, the new Governor made a speech:

… Governor Phillip advanced, and addressing first the private soldiers, thanked them for their steady good conduct on every occasion; an honour which was repeated to them in the next general orders. He then turned to the convicts, and distinctly explained to them the nature of their present situation …[48]

Having told the convicts what he expected of them, the Governor ended on a note of optimism:

Governor Phillip concluded his address, by

---

47 Ibid.
48 Ibid., 66.

declaring his earnest desire to promote the happiness of all who were under his government, and to render the settlement in New South Wales advantageous and honourable to his country.[49]

The extension of the colony came as a surprise to David Collins. He described the ceremony as follows:

As soon as the hurry and tumult necessarily attending the disembarkation had a little subsided, the governor caused His Majesty's commission, appointing him to be his captain-general and governor in chief in and over the territory of New South Wales and its dependencies, to be publicly read, together with the letter patent for establishing the courts of civil and criminal judicature in the territory, the extent of which, until this publication of it, was but little known, even among ourselves.[50]

Neither Hunter nor King mentioned the ceremony. King was busy preparing to leave for Norfolk Island, and may

---

49 Ibid., 67.

50 Collins, *An Account of the English Colony in New South Wales*, 6.

not have attended.[51] Bradley and Tench both described the parade, the assembly of the convicts, Collins reading the commission, and the establishment of the courts.[52]

Legal and constitutional significance

The ceremony on 7 February 1788 observed all the formalities to establish the new colony: the assembly of the entire colony; the reading of the governor's Commission; the appointment of the Governor and the Lieutenant Governor; the assertion of the enlarged territorial limits of the colony; the assertion of the nature and extent of the occupation; the establishment of the courts and the appointment of their officers; and an inspirational address from the Governor.

None of these things had happened at the drinks party on 26 January 1788. After comparing the party on 26 January with the solemn ceremony on 7 February, it is difficult to see how anyone could argue that the party on 26 January 1788

---

51 King, *The Journal of Philip Gidley King: Lieutenant, Rn 1787–1790*, 40. Hunter, *An Historical Journal of Events at Sydney and at Sea 1787–1792*.

52 William Bradley, *A Voyage to New South Wales the Journal of Lieutenant William Bradley Rn of Hms Sirius 1786–1792* (Sydney: The Trustees of the Public Library of New South Walse in association with Ure Smith Pty Ltd, 1969), 80. Watkin Tench, *Sydney's First Four Years Being a Reprint of a Narrative of the Expedition to Botany Bay and a Complete Account of the Settlement at Port Jackson* (Sydney: Library of Australian History, 1979), 41.

had legal or constitutional significance. That notion could be laid to rest, but for Sir Victor Windeyer having delivered a speech in 1961 in which he said that the ceremony on 26 January 1788 marked the foundation of the colony of New South Wales, and the 'reassertion and … making good of the title of the British Crown to the territory of which Cook had already formally taken possession in the name of the King.'[53]

Sir Victor Windeyer's opinion commands great respect. He was a Justice of the High Court of Australia. He also taught legal history at Sydney University, and wrote up his lectures in *Lectures on Legal History*, first published in 1938 and followed by a second edition in 1957.[54]

Justice Windeyer's speech was a response to 'a suggestion by Doctor Currey that 7th February might be celebrated as the anniversary of the foundation of Australia instead of the 26th January.'[55] Dr CH Currey was a legal historian. In 1957, he had published a paper entitled *An Argument for the*

---

53 Windeyer, '"A Birthright and Inheritance" the Establishment of the Rule of Law in Australia', 637.

54 *Lectures on Legal History*, Second ed. (Sydney: The Law Book Company of Australasia Limited, 1957). Sir Victor's book was of its time: it devoted 36 chapters to the history of the law of England; one chapter to the introduction of English law into Australia; no chapters to the development of Australian law; and ended its coverage in the 1880s.

55 '"A Birthright and Inheritance" the Establishment of the Rule of Law in Australia', 638.

Observance of Australia Day on the Seventh Day of February and An Account of the Ceremony at Sydney Cove February 7, 1788. Currey's thesis was:

> … that the 7th February, not the 26th January, should be the date of the annual celebration, throughout the Commonwealth, of Australia Day, and that, for those who would re-enact the major events of a memorable day, the seventh day of February, 1788, was much richer in historically significant incidents and was much more colourful than was the twenty-sixth day of January next preceding it.[56]

Currey supported his argument with the evidence already given in this paper. He added that the documents read at the ceremony 7 February 1788 would resonate with all Australians as:

> … testimony to the transference to this continent of that English law and those principles of public action which are so basic a feature of our Constitution today. That law and

---

56 Charles Herbert Currey, 'An Argument for the Observance of of Australia Day on the Seventh of Day of February and an Account of the Ceremony at Sydney Cove February 7, 1788', *Royal Australian Historical Society Journal and Proceedings* 43 (1957): 153.

those principles are a part of a heritage common to all Australians. They constituted the underpinning of the Government inaugurated here on February 7, 1788. That day is, therefore, a day on which all Australians, regardless of their antecedents or State boundaries, may unfeignedly remember their inheritance as British subjects and celebrate accordingly. Such a day may very fittingly be designated Australia Day.[57]

Justice Windeyer's arguments

Justice Windeyer made three arguments:

1. English law became the territorial law of the colony on 18 January 1788, as soon as the first ship of the First Fleet arrived at Botany Bay;

2. the party for the officers on *Supply* on 26 January 1788 marked the foundation of the colony; and

3. the ceremony on 7 February 1788 was 'in

---

57 Ibid., 172.

law … no more than the proclamation of
an already established fact.'[58]

When did English law become the territorial law of the colony?

This first question was answered by the, 'old and well-known principle of the common law that Englishmen going out to found a colony carried the law with them to their new home.' According to the common law, the allegiance of subjects to their sovereign was personal: 'wherever they went, men were bound by their allegiance and carried the law of their allegiance with them as a personal law. It was their birthright.'[59]

For this part of his argument, Windeyer relied on the chapter by Richard Latham in Keith Hancock's 1937 *Survey of British Commonwealth Affairs.*[60] Hancock was the leading Australian historian of the 1930s. Latham was the Victorian Rhodes Scholar for 1931, a Fellow of All Souls College and the son of Sir John Latham, who became Chief Justice of Australia. Richard Latham would be better known had he

---

58 Windeyer, '"A Birthright and Inheritance" the Establishment of the Rule of Law in Australia', 638.

59 Ibid., 636.

60 W. K. Hancock, *Survey of British Commonwealth Affairs* (London: Oxford University Press, 1937).

not died on active service with the RAF in 1943.

Latham's part of the argument ran as follows: 'When Englishmen found a colony in an uninhabited or savage country, they carry with them the English law so far as it is applicable.' New South Wales was known to be inhabited, but it was held to be *terra nullius* because it was a 'savage country'.[61] The position in Australia went by analogy with the practice in North America, where 'territory inhabited by American Indians was reckoned uninhabited.' Latham did not explain how or why inhabited land could be 'reckoned' to be uninhabited, nor did he mention the decisions of Chief Justice Marshall rejecting the validity of the 'reckoning'.[62] Latham's conclusion was that, when English settlers carried the personal law of their allegiance with them across the world and established a colony in territory known to be inhabited, but 'reckoned' to be uninhabited:

> ... as soon as the original settlers had reached
> the colony, their invisible and inescapable cargo
> of English law fell from their shoulders and

---

61 Governor Phillip's instructions included directions to live 'in amity and kindness' with the indigenous peoples: Instructions given by King George III to Governor Phillip on 25 April 1787: *Historical Records of Australia*, Volume 1, Series 1, pages 13–14. *Terra nullius* = land belonging to no-one.

62 *Johnson v M'Intosh* 21 US [1823] USSC 22; *Cherokee Nation v Georgia* 30 US [1831] USSC 6 and *Worcester v Georgia* 31 US [1832] USSC 39.

attached itself to the soil on which they stood. Their personal law became the territorial law of the colony. Subsequent settlers did not, like the founders, bring with them the law of England as they left it, but entered on the colony as they would into any other country, becoming subject to the established territorial law.[63]

Justice Windeyer said that this passage 'happily described' the principle.

Windeyer referred, finally, to Blackstone's statement that: '… if an uninhabited country be discovered and planted by English subjects all the English laws then in being, which are the birthright of every English subject, are immediately in force'; and to the decision of the Privy Council in *Cooper v Stuart*, holding that, when a tract of territory 'practically unoccupied, without settled inhabitants or settled law' was 'peacefully annexed to the British dominions … the law of England must … become from the outset the law of the colony.'[64]

He continued:

---

63 Hancock, *Survey of British Commonwealth Affairs*, 516–517. *Historical Records of Australia*, Volume 1, Series 1, pages 13–14.

64 Windeyer, '"A Birthright and Inheritance" the Establishment of the Rule of Law in Australia', 636. *Cooper v Stuart* (1889) UKPC 1 at [11]; (1889) LR 14 App Cas 286 at 291.

> The first question then is, at what date is it to be said that in law Australia was first planted by British subjects, to use the old phrase. For more than a hundred years New South Wales lawyers have been able to find a ready answer in the Supreme Court Calendar, which listed 26th January as a court holiday, describing it as the 'foundation of the colony.'[65]

The legal authorities all pointed the same way. English law became the territorial law of the colony of New South Wales 'as soon as the original settlers had reached the colony' (Latham); 'from the outset' (the Privy Council); or 'immediately' the country was 'planted by English subjects' (Blackstone). English law fell from their shoulders and attached itself to the soil on which they stood (Latham).

That happened on 18 January 1788, as soon as a member of the crew of *Supply* set foot on the shore of Botany Bay.

Justice Windeyer was stating the law as it was understood in 1961. The law he stated was an extension of the practice of the European states. It rested on premises that, before 1788, the Australian continent was an 'uninhabited or savage country' and its inhabitants were 'backward peoples.' These premises were racist. They rested, not on evidence, but on the legal fiction that 'reckoned' North America and

---

65 Ibid., 636–637.

Australia to be uninhabited before English settlers arrived. The fiction was an assumption of law so powerful that it could not be overturned, even when there was evidence to falsify it.[66]

It was one thing for English common law to declare that the allegiance of the colonists to their monarch was personal, and a birthright – they were matters matter between the colonists and their sovereign. It was quite another to assert that, when English settlers colonised an 'unsettled' country, English law travelled with them, took root in the soil of the new colony, and became the territorial law of the colony. That affected the existing inhabitants of the colony, making them subject to the common law of England and subjects of the monarch, all without their consent. This was presumptuous just as the European state practice of appropriating the territory of 'backward peoples' was presumptuous.

Both practices – the imposition of English law and European state practice of appropriating the territory of 'backward peoples' – gave colonisation a legal foundation and justification. They permitted the appropriation of territories and the imposition of the common law without the consent of the indigenous inhabitants. They rested on a theory – now discredited – that the indigenous inhabitants of territories

---

66 *Milirrpum v Nabalco Pty Limited* (1971) 17 FLR 141, Blackburn J at 267; and *Mabo [No 2]*, Brennan J at 38–39.

like Australia were, 'barbarous or unsettled or without a settled law.'[67]

Mabo v Queensland [No 2] (1991–1992) 175 CLR 1

The discredited theory that the indigenous inhabitants of Australia were, 'barbarous or unsettled or without a settled law' was the doctrinal justification for: (i) the settlement of British colonies in Australia; (ii) the reception of the British law as the territorial law of the colonies; and for (iii) disregarding the rights and interests of indigenous Australians in their traditional lands. *Mabo* was concerned only with the third of these outcomes.

The plaintiffs in *Mabo* did not challenge British settlement. Nor did they challenge the reception of English law in the colony, or the corollary of its reception: that Australian Aborigines unwillingly and unknowingly became the subjects of a British monarch. Justice Brennan held:

> Thus the theory which underpins the application of English law to the Colony of New South Wales is that English settlers brought with them the law of England and that, as the indigenous inhabitants were regarded as

67 *Mabo [No 2]*, Brennan J at 37–38.

barbarous or unsettled or without settled law, the law of England including the common law became the law of the Colony (so far as it was locally applicable) as though New South Wales were 'an uninhabited country … discovered and planted by English subjects.' The common law thus became the common law of all subjects within the Colony who were equally entitled to the law's protection as subjects of the Crown. Its introduction to New South Wales was confirmed by s24 of the *Australian Courts Act* 1828 (Imp).[68]

In this way, indigenous Australians, 'became British subjects owing allegiance to the Imperial Sovereign entitled to such rights and privileges and subject to such liabilities as the common law and applicable statutes provided.'[69]

Justice Brennan had quite a different view of those parts of the common law of England that would strip the indigenous people of their land rights. When it came to these, he found that the common law was as adaptable as ever:

The facts as we know them today do not fit the 'absence of law' or 'barbarian' theory

---

68 *Mabo [No 2]*, Brennan J at 37–38.

69 *Mabo [No 2]*, Brennan J at 38.

underpinning the colonial reception of the common law of England. That being so, there is no warrant for applying in these times rules of the English common law which were the product of that theory. It would be a curious doctrine to propound today that, when the benefit of the common law was first extended to Her Majesty's indigenous subjects in the Antipodes, its first fruits were to strip them of their right to occupy their ancestral lands. Yet the supposedly barbarian nature of indigenous people provided the common law of England with the justification for denying them their traditional rights and interests in land ...[70]

In the result, *Mabo* confirmed that British settlement imposed English law on the indigenous population and made them British subjects owing allegiance to the Imperial Sovereign but it did not extinguish their entitlement to their traditional lands.

Chief Justice Mason made the position clear in *Walker v The State of New South Wales* [1994] HCA 64, when he held that: 'There is nothing in the recent decision in *Mabo v Queensland [No 2]* to support the notion that the Parliaments of the Commonwealth and New South Wales lack legislative

---

70 *Mabo [No 2]*, Brennan J at 39.

competence to regulate or affect the rights of Aboriginal people, or the notion that the application of Commonwealth or State laws to Aboriginal people is in any way subject to their acceptance, adoption, request or consent.'[71]

Hence, *Mabo* did not impugn Justice Windeyer's conclusion that English law became the territorial law of the colony of New South Wales on 18 January 1788, as soon as members of the crew of *Supply* set foot on land at Botany Bay.

When was the colony of New South Wales founded?

As to the date of foundation of the colony, Justice Windeyer wrote:

> For more than a hundred years New South Wales lawyers have been able to find a ready answer in the Supreme Court Calendar, which listed the 26th January as a court holiday, describing it as the 'foundation of the Colony.'[72]

---

71 At [2]. See also: *Coe v The Commonwealth of Australia* (1979) 53 ALJR 403 at 408 'The aboriginal people are subject to the laws of the Commonwealth and of the States and Territories in which they respectively reside', per Gibbs CJ at 408.

72 Windeyer, '"A Birthright and Inheritance" the Establishment of the Rule of Law in Australia', 636–637.

Justice Windeyer claimed that the drinks party was more than a symbolic gesture: 'The display of the flag and the demonstration under it were intended as a reassertion and a making good of the title of the British Crown to the territory of which Cook had already formally taken possession in the name of the King.'[73]

The problem is that none of the eyewitnesses recorded that anything was said or done along those lines. Moreover, there was no need to reassert the claim that Cook had already made. All that Cook's claim required to make it good was actual occupation of the territory. Finally, Phillip's commission did not require him to 'make good' the title of the British Crown to the territory claimed by Cook. It required him to claim, instead, a larger territory. That claim did require a formal ceremony – which did not take place until 7 February 1788.

Justice Windeyer regarded the drinks party as a demonstration that 'spelt thankfulness, determination and hope – the long voyage of more than eight months ended, safe arrival, the site of the settlement decided, a continent claimed a new enterprise begun.'[74] That was true enough, but it was not a reason to treat it as the foundation of the colony.

The judge made the point that that the drinks party did not mark the introduction of English law: 'No formality

73 Ibid., 637.

74 Ibid.

was needed to make the law of England the law of the new colony. Yet how better could that have been marked than by that ceremony and those cheers that disturbed the ancient silence of the little cove with its tall gums and stream of fresh water fourteen thousand miles from Home?'[75]

There is a ready answer to the judge's question. The introduction of English law would have been far better marked by a formal ceremony, at which:

1. the constituent documents of the colony were formally read;

2. to the entire personnel of the colony;

3. the civil and criminal courts were declared open;

4. possession was claimed of the extended boundaries of the colony, and

5. the officers of the colony were confirmed in their designated roles and positions.

That happened on 7 February 1788. It did not happen on 26 January 1788.

75 Ibid.

Justice Windeyer's claim that the drinks party marked the foundation of the colony of New South Wales is not supported. The colony was founded at the ceremony on 7 February 1788.

The documents establishing the colony

Justice Windeyer based his argument on the operation of English common law. The question of when the colony was founded could also be answered by reference to the documents establishing the colony. The relevant documents are Governor Phillip's two commissions and his instructions.[76]

Phillip's commissions

Phillip's first commission was a military commission, given in October 1786. It was a simple, one-page document, signed by the King:

> We, reposing especial trust and confidence in your loyalty, courage, and experience in military affairs, do, by these presents, constitute and appoint you to be Governor of our territory called New South Wales [on the

76 *Historical Records of Australia*, Volume 1, Series 1: first commission, page 1; second commission, page 2; and instructions, page 9.

enlarged boundaries, already described] and of all towns, garrisons, castles, forts, and all other fortifications or other military works which now are or may hereafter be erected upon this said territory. You are therefore carefully and diligently to discharge the duty of Governor in and over our said territory.[77]

Phillip was invited to make suggestions on his commission and instructions. His suggestions emphasised that the settlement would be more than a military settlement. Phillip wanted instructions covering issues as diverse as: the welfare of the convicts, especially the females; the availability of medical care; the treatment of the natives and the desirability of befriending them; the need to reward and punish convicts and to encourage them to marry; the prohibition of slavery; land grants, and the need to encourage agriculture.[78]

A second commission was executed and delivered on 2 April 1787. It was a civil commission, running to 6 A4 pages in modern print. It began:

Wee reposing especial trust and confidence in the prudence courage and loyalty of you the said

77 Ibid., Volume 1, Series 1, page 1.

78 *Historical Records of New South Wales*, ed. FM Bladen (Sydney: C Potter Government Printer), Volume 1, Part 2, page 50ff.

Arthur Phillip ... do constitute and appoint you the said Phillip to be our Captain-General and Governor-in-Chief of our territory called New South Wales.[79]

The second commission gave Phillip both civil and military powers. It authorised him, for example, to appoint justices and officers of the law, to take and administer the oaths of office, to pardon convicts, to provide for the mentally ill, to levy armed forces, to build fortifications, to grant land and to control commerce.[80]

Phillip's instructions

Phillips instructions, executed on 25 April 1787, descended into detail. They directed Phillip, *inter alia*, to purchase wine, to purchase grain and livestock and to conserve the breeding stock, to establish public stores, to cultivate flax, to explore the coast, to protect the natives, to encourage religious observance, to grant lands to emancipated convicts and to assist the grantees.[81]

The instructions included the following order, telling Phillip to inaugurate the new colony with a solemn ceremony

---

79 *Historical Records of Australia*, Volume 1, Series 1, page 2.

80 Ibid., page 2ff.

81 Ibid., page 9ff.

at which his commission was read and published:

> You are, therefore, to fit yourself with all
> convenient speed, and to hold yourself in
> readiness to repair to your said command, and
> being arrived, to take upon you the execution
> of the trust we have reposed in you, as soon as
> conveniently may be, with all due solemnity to
> cause our said commission under our Great Seal
> of Great Britain constituting you our Governor
> and Commander-in-Chief as aforesaid to be
> read and published.[82]

Phillip's commission was read and published at the
ceremony on 7 February 1788. It was not mentioned at the
drinks party on 26 January 1788.

Justices Deane and Gaudron took up this point in their
judgment in *Mabo*:

> ... it was the intention of the Crown that
> the establishment of sovereignty ... would be
> effected when, after the arrival of the First
> Fleet, Phillip complied with his Instructions
> and caused his second commission to be read

---

82 Ibid., page 9.

and published 'with all due solemnity'.[83]

They added a footnote that: 'The Commission was so read and published on 7 February 1788.'[84]

Justices Deane and Gaudron dealt separately with the question of when English common law was introduced into the new colony. After referring to the authorities about British settlers bringing the common law with them, they said:

> It follows that, once the establishment of the Colony was complete on 7 February 1788, the English common law adapted to meet the circumstances of the new Colony, automatically applied throughout the whole of the Colony as the domestic law ... [85]

What legal or constitutional significance attaches to the events of 26 January 1788?

It is, at last, possible to give a firm answer to this question. The events at Sydney Cove on 26 January 1788 did not mark

---

83 *Mabo v Queensland [No 2]* (1991–1992) 175 CLR 1, Deane and Gaudron JJ at 78.

84 Ibid., 78, footnote 93.

85 Ibid., 80.

the foundation of the colony of New South Wales. Still less did they mark the founding of Australia.

The colony of New South Wales was founded on 7 February 1788. English common law probably became the domestic law of the colony on 18 January 1788, when *Supply* arrived in Botany Bay, but it was certainly the law by the time the colony was founded on 7 February 1788.

The drinks party on 26 January 1788 had no legal or constitutional significance. It was a pleasant interlude for the officers and crew of *Supply* to celebrate their safe arrival in Sydney and to toast the success of the colony they were about to establish.

Founding Australia?

This leaves unanswered the broader question whether the arrival of white settlers marked the founding of Australia.

The Talmage painting has attracted many interpretations. The first was that of the artist himself, who, by calling it *The Founding of Australia by Capt. Arthur Phillip RN Sydney Cove Jan 26th 1788*, asserted that Governor Phillip and a handful of sailors and marines 'founded' Australia at a ceremony at Sydney Cove on 26 January 1788.

The Tate Gallery gives quite a different interpretation of the painting. In the on-line biography of Algernon Talmage on its website, it writes:

The painting depicts the moment Governor Phillip (in the centre of the painting) proposed a toast to King George III, on the evening of January 1788, the day that the Fleet moved from Botany Bay to Sydney Cove. The painting is a celebration of [the] righteousness and importance of colonisation, and a statement of the power of the British Empire.[86]

Mark Latham said this of the painting in his inaugural speech in the Legislative Council:

It depicts the decisive moment in Australian history – the landing of the First Fleet at Sydney Cove on 26 January 1788. The great painting by Algernon Talmage is called *The Founding of Australia*, a founding marked by the arrival of Western civilisation on this continent. It is an appropriate entrance statement for this place, the mother of legislative power and progress in Australia.[87]

Another former Labor leader, Luke Foley said this about

---

86 https://www.tate.org.uk/art/artists/algernon-talmage-2020, visited 15 June 2020.

87 *Hansard, New South Wales Legislative Council*, 8 May 2019.

the painting in his inaugural speech:

> It depicts Governor Arthur Phillip and crew
> on 26 January 1788. The Union Jack flies
> between six tree stumps. Only minutes after
> the arrival of the Europeans, the land clearing
> had begun.[88]

The painting ignored the fact that the country had been in indigenous hands for millennia before 26 January 1788. It included no hint that Sydney Cove was Gadigal land. Indeed, it ignored the indigenous people entirely. It suggested by its title and appearance that Australia only came to life with European settlement. So complete is the symbolism of the painting that it would stand as a perfect symbol of the name that many indigenous Australians give to 26 January 1788 – Invasion Day.

It is an inescapable paradox that 26 January 1788 has come to signify, at once, the arrival in Australia of Western civilisation, of British settlement and institutions, and the dispossession of the indigenous people. Stan Grant has written powerfully about how this paradox has affected him as an Aboriginal man:

> I am a product as much, if not more, of the

88 Ibid., 1 September 2010.

European Enlightenment (which belongs to all of us, not just to the West) as I am of the Dreaming. I value reason; the triumph of science over superstition; the universality of humanity. That I don't accept as fact the myth of the Rainbow Serpent doesn't make me less Aboriginal. I don't believe in the literal interpretation of Genesis either, but I can see the power of the metaphor. I can see the beauty and power of the Dreaming stories – and of the Bible, the Koran, the Mahayana sutras, the Upanishads, and the *Iliad* and the *Odyssey*. I don't seek or need any endorsement from a community to tell me who I am; I don't try to profit from being Aboriginal – I take my skills and expertise to the marketplace, not my identity. I don't want to be put into any box; but rather, as Immanuel Kant said, to live free from 'the ball and chain of an everlasting permanent minority'.[89]

The various interpretations of Talmage's painting highlight the paradox. It is also evident in *Mabo*. The *terra nullius* doctrine was the doctrinal justification for the

89 Stan Grant, *The Australian Dream: Blood, History and Becoming* (Melbourne: Black Inc., 2016), 52–53.

introduction of the English law in Australia. The doctrine is shameful, but what it brought – English law – is valuable. It is shameful that white settlement led to the dispossession of Stan Grant's ancestors, but he is a product of European Enlightenment. It is shameful that Britain exported its petty criminals to penal colonies in Australia, but the colonies are now things of beauty.

Reconciliation

No nation is without events in its past that it would rather had not happened. There were slaves in the United States 155 years ago. Jews were persecuted across Europe 85 years ago. There was apartheid in South Africa 30 years ago. A wall separated East Germany from West 30 years ago. Great Britain and Ireland were engaged in a terrorist war 20 years ago. These are not disreputable Third World countries. They are leading nations of the Western World, and they have mistreated their own citizens in shameful ways, for the most part, in living memory.

That advanced and admired nations have recently mistreated their own citizens does not absolve Australia's treatment of its Aboriginal citizens, but it does raise the question: how do great nations recover from such disasters?

Abraham Lincoln's second inaugural address described the descent into Civil War: 'Both parties deprecated war, but one of them would make war rather than let the nation survive, and the other would accept war rather than let it perish, and the war came.' The severity of the war shocked everyone: 'Both read the same Bible and pray to the same God, and each invokes his aid against the other.'

Victory had not yet come to the Union, but soon would. Lincoln saw that, with peace, the warring parties would need to co-exist once more, and that the burden of the reconciliation would fall on the victorious north:

> With malice towards none, with charity to all, with firmness in the right as God gives us to see the right, let us strive on to finish the work we are in, to bind up the nation's wounds, to care for him who shall have borne the battle and for his widow and his orphan, to do all which may achieve and cherish a just and lasting peace among ourselves and with all nations.[90]

The burden of reconciliation falls on those who come through the crisis in better shape. It is for them to put aside malice; it is for them to take up charity; it is for them to take up the task of binding up the nation's wounds.

90 Abraham Lincoln, Second Inaugural Address, 4 March 1865. The Civil War ended a month later, on 9 April 1865. Lincoln was assassinated on 15 April 1865.

If 26 January remains on the national calendar, it should be as a day of reconciliation.

When, or what, should we celebrate as Australia Day?

If the idea of Australia Day is to celebrate the arrival of British settlers, Governor Phillip arrived in Australia on 18 January 1788, eight days before the events depicted in the Talmage painting. Phillip himself chose to mark the first arrival of British settlers in Sydney Cove, which took place on 24 January 1788.[91]

If the idea of Australia Day is to celebrate the inception of British institutions in Australia, Phillip's government was inaugurated on 7 February 1788, twelve days after the events depicted in the Talmage painting, when Phillip held a formal ceremony to read his commissions and establish the institutions of the colony of New South Wales.

If the idea of Australia Day is to celebrate the foundation of the colony of New South Wales as the first British colony in Australia, it is only reasonable to ask: why would the citizens of other colonies celebrate the foundation of New

---

91 Phillip's commemoration of the landing in Sydney Cove on 24 January 1788 was on a copper plaque in the first Government House. The plaque is now in the Mitchell Library: Call number LR22.

South Wales, when it would never occur to the citizens of New South Wales to celebrate the foundation of any other colony?

If the idea of Australia Day is to celebrate the foundation of the Commonwealth of Australia, we can celebrate it on the anniversary of its foundation: 1 January.

If the idea of Australia Day is to celebrate the inclusion of all Australians in an Australian dream, why celebrate it on the day that indigenous Australians remember as marking the start of the process that separated them from their lands? Calling 26 January Invasion Day, Mourning Day or Survival Day reflects the pain of their dispossession.[92]

If the idea of Australia Day is to celebrate the diversity of our migrant population, why celebrate it on a day that has possible meaning only for British settlers?

Let it be supposed that the national day of a country should celebrate events that reflect the country's values, ambitions, and aspirations. In what sense do the events of the evening of 26 January 1788 reflect Australia's values, ambitions, and aspirations?

Inclusion demands a better response.

---

92 It also balances the narrative which, too often, ignores the indigenous perspective.

Bibliography

150 Years of Australian Art, National Art Gallery of New South Wales.

Catalogue of the State Library of New South Wales.

Hansard, New South Wales Legislative Council.

Historical Records of Australia. Edited by Frederick Watson. Melbourne 1914.

Historical Records of New South Wales. Edited by FM Bladen. Sydney: C Potter Government Printer.

Anonymous. *The Voyage of Governor Phillip to Botany Bay with an Account of the Establishment of the Colonies of Port Jackson & Norfolk Island* London: John Stockdale, 1789.

Bradley, William. *A Voyage to New South Wales The Journal of Lieutenant William Bradley RN of HMS Sirius 1786–1792.* Sydney: The Trustees of the Public Library of New South Walse in association with Ure Smith Pty Ltd, 1969.

Cameron-Ash, Margaret. *Lying for the Admiralty.* Sydney: Rosenberg Publishing Pty Ltd, 2018.

Clancy, Robert. *The Mapping of Terra Australis.* Sydney: Universal Press Pty Limited, 1995.

Clark, C.M.H. *A History of Australia, Volume 2: New South Wales and Van Diemen's Land 1822–1838.* Melbourne: Melbourne University Press, 1968.

————. *A History of Australia, Volume 3: The Beginning of an Australian Civilization 1824–1851.* Melbourne: Melbourne University Press, 1973.

Clendinnen, Inga. *Dancing with Strangers.* Melbourne: Text Publishing, 2003.

Collins, David. *An Account of the English Colony in New South Wales*. Sydney: AH & AW Reed 1975.

Cook, Captain James. *The Journals of Captain James Cook on his Voyages of Discovery: The Voyage of the Endeavour 1768–1771*. Edited by J.C. Beaglehole. Great Britain: The Boydell Press in association with Hordern House, Sydney, 1955.

Currey, Charles Herbert. 'An Argument for the Observance of of Australia Day on the Seventh of Day of February and An Account of the Ceremony at Sydney Cove February 7, 1788'. *Royal Australian Historical Society Journal and Proceedings* 43 (1957): 153–174.

Deakin, Alfred. *Federated Australia*. Melbourne: Melbourne University Press, 1968.

Grant, Stan. *The Australian Dream: Blood, History and Becoming*. Melbourne: Black Inc., 2016.

Hancock, W.K. *Survey of British Commonwealth Affairs*. London: Oxford University Press, 1937.

Hunter, John. *An Historical Journal of Events at Sydney and at Sea 1787–1792* Sydney: Angus & Robertson, 1968.

Inglis, K.S. 'Australia Day'. *Australian Historical Studies* 13, no. 49 (1967): 20–41.

Irving, Helen. *The Centenary companion to Australian federation*. Cambridge ; Melbourne: Cambridge University Press, 1999.

King, Philip Gidley. *The Journal of Philip Gidley King: Lieutenant, RN 1787–1790*. Sydney: Australian Documents Library, 1980.

La Nauze, JA. 'The Name of the Commonwealth of Australia'. *Australian Historical Studies* 15 (1971): 59–71.

Mackaness, George. *Admiral Arthur Phillip: Founder of New South Wales 1738–1814*. Sydney: Angus & Robertson Limited 1937.

Martin, A.W. *Henry Parkes: A Biography.* Melbourne: Melbourne University Press, 1980.

Moore, Bruce (ed). *The Australian National Dictionary Australian Words and their Origins.* Melbourne: Australian National University and Oxford University Press, 2016.

O'Brien, Eris. *The Foundation of Australia (1786–1800) A Study in English Criminal Practice and Penal Colonization in the Eighteenth Century.* Sydney: Angus and Robertson, 1950.

Scott, Ernest. 'Taking Possession of Australia – The Doctrine of "Terra Nullius" (No-Man's Land)'. *Royal Australian Historical Society Journal and Proceedings* 26 (1940): 1–19.

Tench, Watkin. *Sydney's First Four Years being a reprint of a narrative of the expedition to Botany Bay and a complete account of the settlement at Port Jackson.* Sydney: Library of Australian History, 1979.

White, John. *Journal of a Voyage to New South Wales.* Sydney: Angus and Robertson, 1962.

Willey, Keith. *When the Sky Fell Down: The Destruction of the Tribes of the Sydney Region 1788–1850s.* Sydney: Collins, 1979.

Windeyer, The Honourable Sir Victor. '"A Birthright and Inheritance" The Establishment of the Rule of Law in Australia'. *(1958–63) 1 Tasmanian University Law Review 635* ((1958–63) 1961): 635–669.

    . *Lectures on Legal History.* Second ed. Sydney: The Law Book Company of Australasia Limited, 1957.

Worgan, George B. *Journal of a First Fleet Surgeon.* Sydney: The Library Council of New South Wales in association with the Library of Australian History, 1978.